Places & Stories

Poetry by Kim R. Stafford:

A Gypsy's History of the World
Braided Apart (with William E. Stafford)
The Granary
Places & Stories

PLACES & STORIES

Kim R. Stafford

Carnegie Mellon University Press

Pittsburgh 1987

Acknowledgments

Thanks to editors of the following publications which first printed some of these poems: *Atlantic, Barnwood, Field, Highway One, Kayak, Limberlost Review, Malahat Review, Northwest Review, Ohio Review, The Oregonian, Plainsong, Poetry Northwest, Seattle Review, Slackwater Review, Stand, Virginia Quarterly Review, Way Out in Idaho, West Coast Review,* and *Willamette Week.*

The author wishes to thank the National Endowment for the Arts for a fellowship that helped in writing this book.

The publication of this book is supported by grants from the National Endowment for the Arts in Washington, D.C., a Federal agency, and by the Pennsylvania Council on the Arts.

Carnegie Mellon University Press books are distributed by Harper and Row, Publishers.

Library of Congress Catalog Number 86-72299
ISBN 0-88748-042-X
ISBN 0-88748-043-8   Pbk.

Contents

II. Starlight Braille

III. After the Barn

I.
Feather Bag, Stick Bag

Bobby Kennedy's Rocker

Up the long rain-aisle of the Hoh
to a patch of firelight, the nightstorm
pounded our three-sided shelter of cedar
carved with names. Hung our packs
on a spike, hung our socks on a line
to smoke, took turns riding a bent-wood
rocking thing of hazel back and forth
as stories went around of work and the road,
of this place and that time, of woman
and man, of hermit and traveler
meeting and departing as water
rattled the kettle to a boil
over the quick flame-swipe.

Midnight, must have been, when a shape
shaggy with rain and bearded like a bear
showed up, would not come close but stood
beyond the flames to point: "It's still here—
no one broke it up for kindling yet."

"Come in!" we said, but
when his hands began to steam
darkness replaced him, a wall of rain
shouting stories for the Hoh.

Feather Bag, Stick Bag

This five strands bear hair in a split match,
this about seeing two at love kindle my heart.
How much you pay to hear the rest?

This willow stick red thread tied
be that song before Eve wore shame,
before God pluck the garden key out Adam's mouth.
How much you pay to hear it all?

That ship, mother, go down singing.
You hold feather of the bird that saw,
hold feather of the bird that told me
how they all sang when water closed.
You pay me now, I sing it.

Feather bag, stick bag, this little bone
worry me honest about my people
waiting for me pull the skein of that road
all the way out my fist and be done.
They wait, I sing, you pay, that road
ravel me out.

Dust and water, winter road. Feather
bag, stick bag, bone bag all I had
when dust and water been my food.
Not so always. This blue scrap
be ribbon silk, and wrapped inside
she hides, she laughs my song.
Your money jangle out why.

Feather bag, stick bag—see this
penny my anvil hammer pounded flat?
This the song I sing about you
if you don't buy my songs.

Hah! Feather bag, stick bag, bone bag.

There Are No Names But Stories

When the anthropologist asked the Kwakiutl
for a map of their coast, they told him
stories: Here? *Salmon gather.* Here?
Sea otter camps. Here *seal sleep.*
Here we say *body covered with mouths.*

How can a place have a name? A man,
a woman may have a name, but they die.
We are a story until we die.
Then our names are dangerous.
A place is a story happening many times.

Over there? We say *blind women*
steaming clover roots become ducks.
We will tell that story for you at
place of meeting one another in winter.
But now is our time for travel. We will
name those stories as we pass them by:

> *place like smoke*
> *loon on roof*
> *small noise of clapping*
> *hollow of stopping*
> *having many canoe-cedars*
> *place of hiding repeatedly*
>   *cedarbark bedding of cradles*
> *mink's grave*
> *insufficient canoe*
> *sound of swans*
> *one turned over covering another*
> *going with tide*
> *hollow thing at rest*
> *hollow of the northwest wind*
> *having everything right*

Thomas Jefferson Provides a List of Words
So Lewis & Clark May Record the Indian Languages
But They Somehow Lose Their Notes
After Returning Home

Ask of all local inhabitants you meet
their own peculiar names for these things:

> *yesterday, today, tomorrow, a day, a month, a year,*
> *spring, summer, autumn, winter, a man, a woman.*

Learn these, that future travelers may easily
converse, and that trade may be accomplished
with all fairness and thrift:

> *father, mother, brother, sister, husband, wife,*
> *son, daughter, the body, the head, the hair.*

Note any outstanding appearances of mineral riches
that may obtrude into your sight, and whether these easily
may be worked from the ground and transported thence:

> *redbird, snake, lizard, butterfly, fish, frog,*
> *mulberry, a vine, tobacco, joy, sorrow.*

Record landmarks for bands of settlers who may
follow in your path; note locations of luxurious
pasture, and probable sites of profitable tillage:

> *to eat, to drink, to sleep, to laugh, to cry,*
> *to sing, to whistle, to smell, to hear, to see.*

Observe the natural prospect of the country, that artists
may later depict from certain vantage points
the beauty of this land and people as they now are:

> *to speak, to walk, to run, to stand, to sit,*
> *to lie down, to smoke a pipe, to love, to hate,*
> *to strike, to kill, to dance, to jump, to fall,*
> *to break, to bend, yes, no.*

Wilma Tells How
They Moved Old Joseph's Bones

They'd planted him first at Wallowa forks
where Nez Perce used to camp, and Old Joseph
he lay there years, sun and snow,
after his kin got driven out.
You been there? Well then you know.
It's always quiet on a north slope
hill. You hear rivers come mix
from west and east.

But then I was a kid running hayfields
crazy all summer when Nez Perce came back
through, and anyone could see
this gravel quarry starting to get made
by where Old Joseph lay under a bunch of stone.

It was late September, yes, cottonwood leaves
kicking down at dawn when someone says
Indians gathering at the forks
like old troubles. See any guns? No,
didn't see any. Just their kind of caravan
going south, moving Old Joseph's bones,
looks like. Got him in a buckboard.

They pulled us out of town, the way
we followed those spotted ponies
in the dust, our line of Model-T cars
not wanting to miss out. My daddy
drove first gear all day
those Indians went so slow. No one
said much except my daddy over his
shoulder once, "Will you look at them?
Will you look. Won't see that
too many times no matter how long
you live"—up past Lostine, past Enterprise,

past Joseph town to the lake, and then
all the horses and cars and us and them
got mixed up, stopping in the afternoon.

There was finding a shovel. There was smoke
and speeches. There was looking at the ground,
and waves hitting on the lake. I was
crazy, I grabbed this tall Indian boy
by the long braids. He pulled me laughing
from my folks between the cars, down under
horses' bellies in deep willow by the water.
He was horse, I was buggy, we didn't know
a word, and I was afraid, I was afraid
to let go.

Shockley

They called him Briar, he called himself
The Christ and drove his crimson Cadillac
at ninety up the curves of the cliff road
to Idaho's heart—home the white chapel
where disciples waited for his flaming mouth
to kiss each word away. Madonna was his mute
mother, and Magdalen the city waitress he brought
back to the fold one Sunday dawn to preach
a sermon on. She wiped her tears away
with braids unraveling, was saved
and shouted as he bellowed clear,
"See! See! See this holy woman raised
from the neon pit of iniquity
below us on the plain, at the far end
of the road I drive. Late last night
I plucked her out from the diner where
she toiled, was coiled in sin,
and brought her up the mountain
brethren to be raised, raised up
to the heights her soul finds capable
with me, by perfecting guidance changed
from what she was to what you see before you
rising, weeping and repentant, purified."

She stayed, she joined, she praised
beyond all others, until word came back
his Cadillac had left the road past midnight
and two brothers brought him wrapped in spotted
white to the vigil of the collect. Three days
to wait and mourn and sing out glory, three nights
they locked the door for only their Lord would break it
wide with flaming hands. But then that dawn of the fourth
where they took up the floor they buried him,
fit the linoleum seamless down, broke
open their church-pod from within,
scattered back to their lives, back to wages

and fever, possession and fear, her apron
to some diner, her hands to that seasonal trade
that ends not, her mouth to piecework and words
not sanctified, to the taxes of love for another's
hunger lip to lip.

Tubby Tells About His Uncle Mike

My uncle rode with the James boys, you
heard, back them days before Jesse's shot,
and Uncle Mike, old fox, dropped the dollars,
give the posse the slip, landed in the mountains.

When I was five and he was beer-soured old
he'd lead, I'd tag along to a shadow
canyon, two big silver sixguns
jangling at his sides. I'd stand

a heart-sized bottle on a stump
at forty feet, then crouch behind his legs
propped wide in the fern. He'd shout,
Come out the door you little coward!

then draw, one flash his hand exploding
six times, sudden still, while he'd
reload, clicking six gold shells in
then blast his left gun empty

quiet as the wind.
How come, I says, you don't
shoot both guns at once?
Fire in his eyes, dead fern

withered to his knees: *Tubby,*
a man with two empty guns
got as much chance in this world
as a naked woman on a busy street.

Followed him home where he hung
his guns on a nail, shriveled
into a chair, sang me by firelight,
I've lived single all my life.

Liberty Dollar

She was single as new silver, her thin
dress easy. He opened windows for a breeze
and taught her to be dancing but be still.
"Must close your mouth, hush, look
through that window: plum tree blossoming,
rain."
    On the dais she was at last
a flame at eighteen chilled to permanence
when he veiled the plaster, put his small
knives away, held out her coat, and she

was gone into America, land of little
mirrors, of one girl calm, a ribbon in her
hair, a year below her face
face-up on the counter, worn smooth,
tarnished, earned, stolen, struck
new in the die, an honest dollar
spent as she grew older.

"I'm sorry," he had called. "Don't
be afraid. You have the face I need,
the face of liberty"—as rain collapsed,
as the tree burst open, as the girl
turned to look.

Her Mother Tells Her

Fine, little Ida. You got both shoes,
all fourteen buttons by yourself. You made
the long blue ribbon straight. This man
makes his camera ready. Winter light shines good
he says this morning. There on your face
his shadow—that's the cold place you feel.
Don't shiver. He doesn't want you shivering.
Play your kantele. I will tell you
when to stop.

In our Finland they want to see you
with the kantele. Play "Winterleaf"
for Oiva. Play "Little Box."
Play the one you like. I know
the kantele is cold. I know.
No use tuning it now. Later we will.

But now be still. With four stones
I prop your rocking chair. There. Now
stop moving your hand. Look up.
Now be still. Be still, little Ida,
be still.

Juliaetta Coffee Blues

My old truck broke down at the edge of town—
I turn the key, she don't make a sound.
I'll be walking along that highway late tonight.
I step into a cafe to pass the time:
Grade B, that's friendly, coffee's a dime,
A cup of sweet coffee stirred with a silver spoon.

Now there's a warmth that's left in a coffee cup
When the coffee's been all drunk up,
So my heart still holds a memory of you.
That sweet black coffee is all drunk dry,
Just the grounds I'm chewing is left behind
And I'm hunched here holding the cold cup
                                                  of my heart.

I put a pack of sugar in my pocket for the road,
Better take two—if only I'd knowed
What a woman can do to a man when he's all alone.
I tried you with sugar, tried you with cream,
Baby, I could use a warm-up, if you know what I mean
Because I'm hunched here holding the cold cup
                                                  of my heart.

That cafe counter is all scrubbed down.
I got to hold a cup now that you left town
And your hand won't reach my way, no more now.
The waitress says, "Honey, it's time to close,"
I start out walking like the wind that blows
Down a street that's dark and lonely as a man can be.

I put a pack of sugar in my pocket for tonight,
Out on the highway when the stars are bright
And that cold wind starts whistling through my bones.
I thought I saw some headlights' far-off glow,
But it's only the moon shining through the snow

Where I'm standing in the gravel trying to hitchhike
                    on the wind.

But there's a warmth that's left in a coffee cup
When the coffee's been all drunk up,
So my heart still holds a memory of you.
That sweet black coffee is all drunk dry,
Just the grounds I'm chewing is left behind
And I'm hunched here holding the cold—

but that's an old story by now,
so old it's just about worn away.

To Elko and Back

1.

When Nyle tops a bar stool
and starts to chant his first
bull ride, the craps game stops
on a dime, his rhyme sparks hot,
and even the pretty sullen mouth
of the dealer pops in blond
surprise. The silver wrangle
of the slots gets stunned to a hush
by his brash bellow—his shady hat
pulled snug, long wire-tip mustache
fairly slavering with honest joy.
And when his poem starts to really wail,
Nyle and the stool quit the floor
sunfishing together in that magic sober
drunk when the chute slaps open, and one
clean ton of bull goes berserk. Gamblers
dash for cover somewhere dark, and our
holy bucaroo dancer of the word goes wild.

2.

Don't tell me on cowboy poetry. My dear dad
broke us all on a ranch, and I've got no beauty
left for that, thank you just the same. Yeah,
your rodeo tramps and waddie hobo bums—
I split for town and prayed to never slip back
soon as sixteen hit and I could live alone legal.
But gentlemen, how about some pie? Sixteen sweet
kinds. I could name them off, or you could say
your pleasure. Coffee for the road?

3.

Everybody said, *She's deaf,*
she'll never talk, and they just
ignored her. But me, I talked at her

all the time, just like she was ordinary
sane. Like she could read my lips, or taste
the vibrations in my meaning clear somehow.
So I guess she must have got to be about
nine—never said a thing to save her life. Then
one day I was talking away at her, she
says all in a rush *That's a god-damned lie!*
And you know, now she's married, got two
kids, living in Idaho, and real happy!

4.

I'm glad to meet you, real
glad to see you, but first, before we
get any further with whatever it is
you want to say, I have a question for you.
You ready? What's your position on federal
gun control? I gotta know that
before we go any further, for if you're
for it, we don't have no more to say.

5.

Oh that Susie's a wild one, someone said
as she poured a bucket of ice and popcorn
over her dancing lover's head. Someone else
opened the door for air, and snow dusted the floor.
The juke pounded like a sweet old headache. Now
Susie called the bartender's wife, Hey June,
let's dare. I dare you climb that pool table
and shiver out of your clothes!

6.

Hey, this the Continental Divide? No? OK. Well,
you know where we can find that Sun Bear Family?
They got Vision Mountain. We been looking

but we missed it. Went past in the dark, I bet.
Trying to lighten our load. Got to keep
the tipi poles, but what else? Kids don't need
toys in the woods. Still got a few books. Need
any? Didn't think so. You look pretty loaded yourself.
We been together seven years. Wintered in the desert
easy. Thought we'd camp in the Blues awhile.
Got friends in there unless they're gone. Got our
seed, looking for ground. Drive careful, brother.

Losing One

Too small to work at haytime
she down by South Fork making
a willow house. At dusk some said
her red ball drifted skittish
too far out. Some said maybe
swimming, maybe sunshine in her eyes.
Some said, now keep her mother home,
now send her father searching the fields.
All women, men, tall children
to seek her body fast at the riffle,
slow through pools, all in a chain
knit hand to hand, at each bank
ankle deep, in the channel to the breast
and gasping at the suck and swirl,
the current burrowing brown from last
night's mountain rain. Swallows dipping,
thunder to the east, not much talk
but *Hold me, Wait, No nothing*
that family tribe—sister, cousin, now
brother, father, mother in the line, flat
gray waterslap, not willing ever
to stop. Chill and mosquitos,
ozone smoke, lightning there
and there, then starlight:
Enough? Not yet. And she
somewhere bumping the long scour
of the riverbed without a word.

Flower Drawn from Thorn

You took me to the mountains
where we stood among the corn.
You covered my mouth and spoke:

> *little straight tree, beautiful and happy,*
> *not yet turned aside to wisdom.*

You led me higher and I looked again:
your face was a tree's wood shattered apart,
a stone the years tore open. My
clothing was a darkness pulled away.

> *little bird, lick water from each bud—*
> *you will be satisfied.*

Stars were thick above me
somewhere. I had not watched the path
for you were leading. Then you left.
There would be no sound. My hands
were knobs of light. I was to be
tamed. You told me this: water
would be ice, and ice clear stone,
and stone the skull protecting God.
The wind passed over. Then
a shape loomed up before me. For this
I rose, and all my trembling fell away
as my clothing had fallen in the corn:
my fingers found a mouth that spoke
and hurt, a blessing from it flowed
over my shoulders, I fell by blood
into the grass for joy.
Carried like a rag, raised up I hung
suspended in her arms. One mouth
served us both, one small song
tangled backward through my teeth.
Claws unraveled my fingers, unraveled
my limbs, crumpled my body and
cleared by burning what I knew,

by the fire of stars opened
my moon-bright head of shell
until my eyes looked inward
for the world was done.

Heavy when I woke against earth,
my hand held a bloom of pain
and dark with the red sweat of life,
its work, its grief. Delight went
through me bone by bone. I longed
for water. Then, when light had come,
you found me, knelt down
beside me with a cup and blanket.
I took them so you would not speak.
I stared into your face.

Natural Wonders

When we hiked in to Hidden Falls
against the ragged Tetons
lonely trappers named

we heard a sound like jet planes
practicing to kill us all but
older than such human work, more

permanent—the fall's roar
through contorted trees
that winter would regain. My love

went up before me on the path, and I
came after around the bend. We found
a woman alone holding her own arms

close, perched on a boulder dark
from spray, her long hair glistening
and loose, her back so bowed

for sorrow or delight—as if
the flash of water dashing down
before her were alive, and she

a white shrub summer left behind.
We drew aside against a stone,
we watched the snowmelt

shattered from the high stream,
restored deep in the pool.
But this was nothing

to the woman rocking the private
cradle of her bones, embrace and pivot
clean, when leaning from herself she

swayed alone. We turned away,
came down, the mountain's chill
burning in us, somehow happy then

to be in danger, to be together, yet
to have our kinship with that woman
dancing in the wilderness.

Later Voyage
of the Trident Submarine

No one knew where we had gone
when the blunt shell of our city
sank through Pacific waves to wander
at our captain's will. We brethren
had left families behind,
we had left government behind—
no president in the ark, no senator
or admiral, tycoon or gambler
this time through—for we were
secret in steel rooms where the quick
slice of water spoke as we went down.

We wore our names in blue thread—
Wolfgang, Ordway, John, and Geoffrey—
practicing again for death. And the fire
at the core of our ship buried one
hundred fathoms under the ice glowed white
but made no sound. We hovered
at the balance depth, gathering
into ourselves the short trill of human
genealogy. Then each man stripped,
climbed into a missile's cradle,
each angel patriot entered a gleaming
tube aimed upward, legs stretched long,
breathless chest made small at this
last purpose of our captain's will.

A hatch above me opened—I rejoiced
spinning out and up through fathoms of cold
where thin light sudden above me
broke the surface, I with many
swarming into the sky, my trajectory bending
west and south toward the heart of Asia,
over the moon's path on water, my continent

dark to the west, no light on it at all
for that was finished.
                    Along the long
ribbon of shoreline I turned slowly
at my steepest peak when my target
beckoned me down, radar guided me
compact with urgency over land
toward my city, the city chosen for
me alone, its tiny ruins vacant,
already destroyed by those
before us, black and twisted city
where I fell face down, a witness
to permanent history I would change.

As the small wings at my shoulders twitched,
as the trigger within me began to chime
I above my city began to drive
each atom outward, one pattern
outward, each syllable of thunder
released beyond sound, each bright
memory shattered plain to fragments
in the final generosity I contained.

Acres of light opened from my body
as light burst from my brethren angels
around the world falling on cities
of their own, where radiant women
sprang back into being, where men rose
whole from despair, where children
woke in their own small cradles of grass
as birdsong broke from solitude
and the city restored became itself
resonant with detail, all citizens

of earth thrust into their oldest gestures
of prayer, into their work, their joy,

even to the blessed confusion
and recklessness that is their life
but with one habit born this time:
do only what the sun, water, a word,
a simple change of heart could heal.

Living by Kindness

Strange things happen in the mind—
like the time I stopped under a streetlight
to write on an envelope a chance thought
furrowing my head—"we haven't all
killed each other yet"—and then went on
through the dark streets of my Idaho city
trudging coaldust and snow.

Next day at the lumberyard, I caught
a clerk glancing at me sideways.
Then I remembered the envelope
in my heart-pocket, its message
bold as a badge: "we haven't
all killed each other yet."

He was good to me.
Sliding a pine plank off the rack
so clean and sweet, so long, he said,
"You paid for an eight,
but all we got today is twelves."

Words have made nothing happen yet
except a free four feet of pine
and the cradle it made
and the child I held
under a light in snow.

"Grandpa, Come On In and Have Some Pie!" But He Always Drove Away

That house in Burley with windows split
and blue door ajar, I know
you've seen it shine or storm, shredded
red curtains billowing loose, the lawn
gone to thistle and purple vetch.

When I was little an old man
used to drive slow past that house,
circle the block and pass again
and again. They say for true he
moved out and into his dented dodge
after his soldier son didn't come back,
after his wife had her stroke and faded
in a day.

Down by the river where he made
his evening fire we saw his charcoal
drawing on the cement trestle wall:
a man in a car, and inside the man
a woman, and inside her a child.
They came together near the face—
one ear shared by two, one mouth
by three.
        Rain washed it all
away by now, and only kids
from out of town who don't know
the story use that house
to get stoned and lie down
together by candlelight.

Dare to Be Great!

The session revved up, glad
shouts ringing out our sudden fame
when the expert moneyman from
far to the East called out, *"Who
among you . . ."* and the fluorescent lights
quit, *"knows . . . ,"* and he faltered,
and a woman answered, "I!" too soon. Lights
came on. We stirred, newly made
in our blue chairs: *"enough to be
GREAT!?"* Questioning darkness, he
in the flash of certainty
flickered.

We'd paid. We stayed
to live this through, as if
dozen days and dollars sputtered
past our glittered eyes
now spent when the lights
went out for good.

We helped each other toward the door
where the exit light burned halo green,
toward the neon parking lot that beckoned
like a clean window through a dollar bill.

If We Shed Our Names

At the heart of our city ants have built
a city of their own small labor, life by life
jostling thick sand into a mound
to turn away rain from their deep home.

They toil inside the steel fence of the transformer
compound, the Power Company's preserve. No-one
walks beyond the Danger sign, unless they carry
a sprig of food or a belly of water.

By noon sun is on them, by October
snow has covered their pyramid.
Their praise returns with spring.
They grow smaller and older than we.

Within their labyrinth, ancient paradise
the size of a footprint, they retreat into the factory
of earth to practice by sleight of hand and scent
intimate politics with juniper and rain.

Salish Graveyard, Central B.C.

When wind flips open her grave-house roof
each hand holds what it owned:
scissors, thimble, sewing machine
wheel that hand wore smooth
still belonging to its cold bones.

All working parts become one,
screws wedded to the steel they held.

Then snow-melt admires metal:
one little shuttle frozen with rust,
its bobbin of black thread sealed inside.

When Saint Babylon Rides Her Midnight

limousine to pick up strangers starved
at the ruby heart of cities no one pays her
any mind, though she spangle her dress of dimes
spilled from slot machines, and jangle
her pretty voice out the window sliding by.

They turn from the glint in her eyes,
from laughter jostled out those little
lips she paints with moon. Saint Babylon
settles back to cruise, tells her husky driver
"One more time down the Avenue, but slow."

About the hour the street-sweeper waggles
at the curb, and cleaning ladies shiver
for their busride home, the last hard
folks who suffered the dizzy sacraments
of hunger, cross-eyed wine, are propped

or fallen on the steps, or tumbled
flat in alleys under a slit of starlight.
Then they hear Saint Babylon stop
her long black ride for the holy
lonely children of the street, hear

her high-heeled slippers step through wine
and shattered glass. Through their delirium
the driver lifts them stiff with cold,
slides them in the back seat easy, that door
closed with a heart-beat snap. She rides

before their startled bodies raised
from their heaps of rags to see
smoldering eyes that snuff out stars,
hair furrowed by rain, and tall bones
bound for distances.

Wild Swans out South Jetty Road

Across the mire-sand straits, in a pool of rain trudge
the Audubon ladies with their gunny sacks of Palouse
wheat for swans pivoting buffeted by wind,
a hundred wintering here because women
are kind, and others stay away.

                         They came in
low over town, October, and the cry went out
to call Aunt Bea. Dunes had shifted, the swan
pool narrowed. Her salt-flecked rusting Dodge
coasted to a stall.

                  Now Bea and Helen, coats
slapping wet, lean on the wind and stride
toward that white congress alert for pleasure
when grain is scattered and our two women
lead a flock of swan-boys round and round.

Paulina Rodeo

There was varnished fiddle's shriek
and startled cry of a dancing woman's
pleasure, then bawl of men calling
each other out—*You Harlan, Roger,*
Wade and Reub, get over here!

There was steady thunder
of a bulldogger's horse gone
pounding out the chute, and sun so hot
beer sweat, and hazed steers
balked even crazier than usual.

There was that fine, fat old bucaroo
guest of honor riding a thin horse slow
around the arena to shake every
grinning man's hand and kiss
every handy woman on the mouth.

But after all that,
there was chill dawn somewhere
west of Suplee when he took his razor
and red bandana down to the stream
to shave, and redwing blackbirds chanted

their watery songs, and lupine
glistened out from hoofprints, and water
shattered from his hands as he peered
cold into the steel mirror
propped fragrant in sage.

Morning Report by Lady Makepeace

When the little town of Fiddle, Idaho,
finally got civilized and ready
to settle down awhile, the mayor
decreed to put in sidewalk
all across in front of his house
so citizens wouldn't longer muddy
their boots coming for the mail,
or to be married, or do the laundromat
with a half a winter of coveralls.
He packed in cement by mule
and did it right in style all
smooth and regular just like
downtown, finishing late one
Saturday night. But Sunday dawn,
after the weekend customs quieted some
and most local critters lay sobering
in sleep, Lady Makepeace on her high-
stepping way to church found that
sidewalk promenade all marred
and permanent with tracks of bear.
You see, she said, *you can't break old
habits with new style in Fiddle, Idaho.*

What Ever Happened to Gypsy Slim

who camped under bare library elms
with his saxophone and little stove:
"Excuse me, mam. I have a question
for your time. You see, I am about
to sauté my onion for the evening
and I wonder what herbs you recommend?"

Shopping cart man who stretched plastic
over that bench carved *Laurence Sterne*,
eccentric danger from another time,
spoke: "I don't care if it's family, friend,
house, job, creed, ethnic group, country,
institution, or sex—they *all* try to stifle
what *you* can be."

But they got him. Pigeons settle
where his cart kept city pavement dry
a few months, and clean citizens
are not afraid to walk on that side
where his raving once made them stop.

Watching the Automatic Typewriter
Reproduce My Vita

Little ball of the alphabet spins
and strikes in a blur, drifting over
vacant pages town to town, house to hermitage,
year to year, job to journey: *shift, stop,*
lock, control, escape, return, clear.

Keys go down, I'm gone again:
Florence, Boville, Port Townsend, Port
Orford, North Powder, Hood River, Joseph,
Pocaloo, Burns—my night bus
route-call trailing a maze
clear back to the first blank
ticket for hunger, toil, and joy.
Always an alley, often a river
by night where fog gentles all trouble
and a dog barks for salvation or change.

It's done.
Roll in another sheet: name, birth,
address, then *shift, control,*
escape, return, clear.

Man Who Stole a Loaf of Bread

And then he said, "When I was hitchhiking
across December flats of Wyoming sage
around midnight I tossed my sleeping bag
over the barb-wire fence, heard it break
through ice and splash: irrigation ditch."

He settled against the battered keyboard
and his eyes turned up in prayer: "God,
the stars were bright that time. Let me
now play 'Silent Night' for you—
the lonely way."

Sound Anthologist

It helps to be blind in this work,
or able to work blind to gather
sound anonymous for film—like old
Homer who could sing it right, because
he couldn't see a thing. It's purity
counts: you go out to crickets
in an Idaho field, to trains
tapering off their wail.

I was in this motel, see, somewhere
down by Twin when I heard the sweet
perfect wind of my life. Not your
antique breeze or storm. This
was the word of God in a blasted
cottonwood right in tune. So I set
the mikes out twenty feet from the car
and let it play. In about seven minutes
it slipped away still.

But when I played it back for the man
from MGM, he stood there like the dog
at the victrola: stunned.
"What happened to the machine?"
he said, then closed his mouth.

Nineteenth Century News

Lacrosse! Lacrosse! Twelve Canadian Gentlemen
vs. Twelve Iroquois Indians:

Blue Spotted
Hickory Wood Split
Pick the Feather
Hole in the Sky
Flying Name
The Loon
Deer House
Crossing the River
Outside the Multitude
Scattered Branches
Great Arm
Wild Wind

On Her Majesty's cricket green.

Beautiful Death

Crescendo of shattered glass,
din of wrenched steel, fire siren
awry, all flashing confusion
and uncle stretched by the highway
dim by starlight, wordless dead
under a stranger's quilt of blue
and white, hump on the gravel him.
Then uncle bedded under a stone
and after, the ambulance driver
mailed the quilt anonymous home,
to be taken out some nights,
shared like a story or song,
some of the color him, some
of the pattern beautiful death,
some rusted face, wedding ring
for him, for us alone a theft
and a gift in one night's work.

Aunt Charlotte Said

Rosemary, this story my daddy
told me when I was your age: Down
by the caves in the canyon his father
said to him, "Don't ever go in. Dark
and cave-slime cover your face.
You might never come out, might never
get dragged out. I didn't raise you
for that, to lie in a narrow slot
stuck silent before you're grown."

But then my daddy was a little older
than you, Rosemary. He found a cave, pulled
a tree aside, went in where only he
on hands and knees could slither deeper
on his belly, could hitch along
after the candle flicker, the plunk
of water somewhere past the tunnel's
bend, breathing all his breath away
deep at the tight place to be
smaller than he was: wispy little
body way down under the cold
rock of the world.   The dark opened
in a room. He wiped mud off his eyes,
held the candle up. On the wall
was a word scrawled the way a child
his own age would write: his father's
little name.
                        Oh his daddy's gone, Rosemary.
And my daddy's gone. But I keep that story.
You remember now: there are two names there
in the dark of the cave, down in the earth
where they were not supposed to go.

II.
Starlight Braille

This Woman Was Our Kite

When she'd had one too many
we heard a small whippoorwill song
and she lifted off hilarious as fog.
When the tallest branches of the elm
didn't snag her loose hair blaze
and missed the petticoat she swirled,
men stood stunned, and children cried,
"Grandmother! Come back before you break!"
But she smiled mindless as a photograph, lost
her dainty slippers, with the dizzy poise
of laughter spun upside down, her
billowing lace unraveling smaller
as she rose toward evening stars.

A white thread trailed over the grass—
"Grab it! Knot the end so she
can't get away!" Her daughter's
knuckles were the spool.

Women called out, "Lady reach wide,
trim your sail, don't fall!"
The long thread tugged at nibbling stars,
wind swung easily around, and she
was a pale spot adrift
on silent constellations of the west.

"Praise the Lord for beauties
of the night!" her sister said.
"Mind of her own and always
had," her husband said. "I'm
letting go," her daughter said.

Hacksaw Says Their Marriage Vows

I am the first part of joinery
in this dividing of self from self,
this opening wedge with a kerf
of light in my slender wake.
I take you down by dust so
fine you will not miss
those old shapes done away
by the marriage of flame to wood
when one voice speaks.

My teeth on the blued steel blade
divide all things, reveal all things,
consume all things, renew all things
to what they were before. For he
must be divided from himself,
and she from herself, to be one
passion kindled right.

Medieval Prayerbook

Where Eve and Adam dazzle unafraid in pleasure,
where the honeysuckle serpent twines asleep
over their kissing feast, the tree of physical
wisdom stands at the still pirouette
of the world's beginning, each leaf
labeled a Latin sin, and water spills
from earth without a word. From the hedge

tendril fingers of a man loosen joyful
some woman's habit from her, opening
the secret terror of perfection Eve
and Adam found, the sweet small garden
below season and belief. A plucked
monk falls from the interlace limbs
of pride. By acorn, clover, yellow

glare butterflies settle licking dew
where green bud banners unfurl *avaritia,*
ira, accidia, gula, inanis gloria. A thrush
perched on the twig of *invidia* sings one hymn
to a pea flower just sprung, while coy sorrow
disguised as a wet rose yields in bloom
to a fox with a red harp, to a jeweled

tambourine, to the gold-crowned maiden
with the fishes twirled from waves, tight swirl
of crows mobbing an owl, to the bright blue
spread of a peacock's pride afire, to all
psalms by the ink of wine embroidered
onto blades of grass. The plowman drives two
oxen over earth, his furrow closing sod.

Saddle an old man—jolly girl jerks the silver
bit between his teeth, her gold hair loose
and the doe-skin reins throttled tight, her
lips laughing a white blossom. Blood bursts

from a stag's throat, from a boar torn
by dogs nuzzling prey, and gentle hunters
frolic with their spears and horn.

Where the moon rising and setting sun
illuminate a woman walking alone
under boughs of medallions named
for secret cruelties in men,
virgin bees amazed from their cathedral
swarm to light her path, her coffin-pod
cast empty where she rose from clay.

Now all are standing holy
where hounds in the garden leap
for the heart-shaped leaf *luxuria,*
and sheaves of the damned are carted off,
the ragged woman beat with staves, the fine
tall lady slain with stones, and the bishop's
dancing daughter burnt for love.

Book of Hours

For the kindling in his touch, her hand
opens so still bobbing grass not jostled
at all, swaying ripe in her dowry pleasure,
turning to her hours of stars, her lit
fingers lifted in praise fevered to serenity:
More and less in the savor they
built intrinsic as bone in me, less

and more where lace-print leaves dyed
my shoulders, less for desire and more
this hour for fear desire would not
come back when called by the bleat
I spoke, when his head a mute
breathing knob rested by mine
and less and more were done.

Stand for pollen, for rain, for each
hour spent, for star light's
gift, the gift of cold she held
out and he took, for the book he
opened and she read with her lips, her
tongue and his, the book she opened
by starlight braille and he knew.

Figurehead of the Good Ship MaryAnne

Her breasts swell to shatter waves
that hid a battered rose bouquet prayer-snug
between her hips. Twin knees dimple
the wet green dress pressed close by wind,
cedar hem scattered like a catspaw
over two red shoes on the prow
bountiful with leaves.

Her black hair billows, her face juts out
so bold the cruelest sailor's tempest would quail
for two eyes crooked of a diverse size, for
that red mouth split at a glint of teeth
where laughter soon, soon will blossom
for the rage of every thousand, thousand
miles cast in tatters off his back,
and the lamp turned low, her shoulders
unfurled, the night-prayer clenched
in her wood hands revealed, where terror sunk
wells up to foam when the century fathom
blue in her quick eyes lights the deep.

Permanent Woman, 1929

1.

Lips more worn than the gown
her shoulders hold, she lives
by the small mouth and spark
bright eyes, by the shine
her hair gives back, black and
silver, by her hands together
receiving the braid's unraveling
in the garret window, the gable
glimmering through fir trees,
and behind the house rounded hills
rising up where clouds about the white
small seal of the moon are still,
the pale road receding from her
room, from the shrine of it all
when the crickets end.

2.

In that lit window through the oaks
his private figure under a lamp lives
magnified, his tiny fingers
polishing the silverware.

With a distant click of small tools working,
muffled pane split open, dead-bolt sprung
the probe-light seeks him down the hall:
prickling garment of sweat.

Reach out for the phone receiver,
for the pistol handle—number, bullet,
heroic sentence lifted from his body
suddenly complete.

By moonrise leaves have fallen,
the old majority. She wakes
and listens hard. Each life pivots
above a boundless generosity.

A Pretty Message of Farewell

Forsaken, obedient, her homing pigeon
beat upward terrified by the two-ounce
camera harnessed throbbing at its breast,
by each discrete explosion of belief:

thin road tossed down dark ravines, blurred
meadow stroked by wind, a pelt of moonlight
over hills, then snow by gravity's
aim sent heartless down, raw tree

stripped clean, map of sparks
his town beams upward every night
as if some unbodied, light-boned soul
might be tempted to settle and suffer

all the dangers of ending flight.

Biology Darkroom

Safelight red and the timer ticking slow
for Donna's fingers in the swirl of fix—
her grandmother's face rocking in the tray
too pale with a smile of burnt silver.
"Dodge the background, burn the eyes in
next time," Donna said.

                  She needed air,
led him out the light-lock double door,
down the corridor dim with specimens:
cats and catfish bundled shelf on shelf,
human bone-rack hung from a wire, forty-four
little pigs in a glass drum. She turned
to face him, her elbow on the sealed pail
marked "human embryo."

Thin in summer clothes,
dazed from the darkroom, she said
"Let's open it." "No," he said.
She studied him, her fingers splayed
across the white tub's belly.

At the rim "To Open, Pry at Slots"
and Donna fought the lip up
slot by slot, slid the cover off
and leaned aside for him.

In water, white tight fists,
clenched face in a breathless privacy.
"Touch her," Donna said.
"She's old enough to have a name."

At Caesar's Palace, Stateline, Nevada

In the twilight of the slot arcade
I know I'm lucky while I live. Whatever the odds
the roving change-man deals me quarters
with a grin. At a pair of vacant bandits
I choose the one with cherries up. I sit.
It has a face, three eyes. I'm generous. I lose.

Then beside me an Indian woman settles in to play
glittering in wristbands beaded red, black
braids and silver crescents at her ears
and throat. Slender in leather
and purple satin, her shoulders sway
with the spangle charm I might
have known, her fingers click in coins
like rain, and her slot is quick to choke
out silver. She's so good she doesn't need
to laugh when quarters spatter
past her hands. Agile grandmothers on a spree
stoop to gather in the bright fish
of pleasure, giggling on their knees
hilarious with envy and surprise.

She waves off the debris of happiness.
Neon eyes—didn't she earn this win
by the tattered gamble of other nights?
She turns away with two good hands' full
at her breasts, and the silver moon
below her ear slunk out of sight,
that garment of her hair so long.

Anna Bollein Queen

Gold-haired lady, whose eyes are distant
as her long age of 29, is well composed,
her gaze cast down, the lace at her throat
held snug by two small bows sketched pale
by Holbein's pencil. Later there would be time
to complete this queen's attire, the thread
that holds her cap pressing a shallow furrow
in the paper-white skin of her neck.

The Restless Calligraphy of the Human Form
in Boundless Varieties of Change

Because hair is a long garment tethered
to the mind, because she is a flame
they could not quench, because
one life is not enough, dance
breaks from the chrysalis
of a woman, all flow, all hinge at hip
and wrist, pliant as fire when it turns
in its path, ever logical by varying:

she drifts into the open,
shimmers on the narrow stairway
music carves from darkness,
her hand's bud unraveling, arms
kindled by a lamp that blossoms
vein by vein, desire rooted
desperately there when the dance
sheds her wild body finally
like smoke from a long burning,
when the lights go down
and music dances from her
in a separate shape away.

In a Photograph My Grandmother, Re-Shingling the Roof, Pretends to Be Departing for Heaven

Wrinkled smile, gloved hands, the minister's
bride grips her saw to rip clouds wide
that bar one tight-mouthed path toward stars,
toward gingham blooming, toward Bible leaves
strewn about, to their hayhouse honeymoon
again, to love beyond sight. She might
with rimless glasses, with a white apron
safety-pinned to her bosom lean
beyond the ladder's last rung,
the roof shattered about her, open
rafters studded with nails, tornado work
of one life winnowed from their
husk house.

His sermons, her diary, their silence:
Nebraska wind passionate about ripe
cottonwood stripped and budded. His seed, her
pod, thunder's vine she rides—gone up
one jagged path of light.

III.
After the Barn

Don't Talk on the Sabbath, She Said: Sing or Be Still.

Its hinges spoke open
where wind came waltzing in
closing the door behind it.

She swayed through the room,
hands clenched on a spoon and a prayer,
humming an old hymn: Jacob's Ladder

in the barn, the loft piled high
for a place to lie snug while
winnowed light filled the building

bowing under the wind, seasons swinging
swallows in and out, grandmother
calling from the house

eighteen years away.

Under an Oak in California

When Hitler kissed the children
and Mussolini played the violin
my father planted spindly cork oak
saplings in the dust of California
because they said this war might
never end. "The nation will need cork
and wood and shade," the foreman said.

He with a crew at an awkward march
over the hills above some snug town
with a saint's name took two steps,
swung his short hoe at the call dividing
earth, and one thin blade of life
from the bag at his belly rooted there,
then the crew lurched forward.

Maybe the rain would come, or maybe
the crew return with water packs.
"Plant many, for many will die," the foreman
said, while Hitler kissed the children
and Mussolini played the violin.

Opening the Book

When our landlord's name was Manlove
and the world was three years old, when
the car wouldn't start and summer was
longer than life and warm with dew
in the soft morning we stepped early
onto the tarred trestle above Tualitin
river water fish nibbled, leaves
flashing between ties Helen counted
for two nephews, who were my brother and me,
and then the parents with the baby between them
singing, *I feel like a morning star.*

On the far side shining grass and dew
we tumbled into the wild orchard deep
with sunlight and spearmint, opened our
blanket to shake out walnuts and bruised
apples, father in the pear calling down
where we were sticky and laughing rolling
late plums into hollows of grass, Helen
pulling down an arc of white roses
so our basket might be filled, mother
humming with bees while my sister slept.

How carefully we walked over the trestle
toward evening, how slow toward winter
and the house that would burn, the strange
changes our bodies would learn and carry
for another sister, for my own child
all our words poured out, and trees
we would hollow into earth and wait
for shade to cover our family
singing *I feel like a morning star.*

How We Live

Possum is like our family
my father said in the dream
when he was away. Old possum
is a world that travels at night,
a house with feet, a steady beast,
one ungainly happiness little ones
cling to. And if one falls off
the possum-world stops on its path
and waits. Trust they all fit.

After the Barn Collapsed

I found the swarm toiling on their comb,
slanted wall slung taut by blackberry rope
rooted to earth. It was May, honeyflow,
and the bees were frantic to taste and spit,
to trample, trade mouth to mouth flowersap
their bodies held for such meeting—all women
but the drones' blunt heads bee-women fed
tongue to tongue.
                    With smoke and water,
with a leaf-brush I coaxed them
into my white box. The barn would burn,
and the place be scraped to raw dirt.
Only a few escaped to finger the wax
print my blade left behind, to hover
where their wall had stood and speak
the buzz twang of despair in the honey month.

Finding the True Point of Beginning

According to Transamerica Title Company
our ground lies in the northwest corner
of an old farm. Before barn-building
it is good to locate the true point
of beginning, a place to measure from,
even if it falls at the heart of blackberry,
abandoned orchard kneeling into thorn.

Commencing at our neighbor's fence
with sledge and cedar stake
trailing the tape behind
I walk north 89° 31′ 30″ west,
threading the thicket of wild plum
where possums feast and ramble by dark—
grass tunnel, scat along the bough.

Unraveling "part of the west ½
of the northeast ¼ of the southwest ¼
of the northwest ¼ section 28 township
1 south range 1 east Willamette Meridian
county of Multnomah state of Oregon"—here
at 96.66 feet, ankle-deep in leaves, tape
taut, stake set, I drive, drive, drive, drive.

Striking home, the stake shatters.
I kneel in an inch of moss, paw
through dirt, touch a ring of rust
on the iron pipe surveyors left in '55.
So they marked this place; so
you and I found it again.
Stay close for awhile.

Like the trees, we are visitors.

Night Work in June

Stumbling out with flashlight and smoke
to check the bees, we passed our apple
ladder dropped flat in deep grass: eight
wet gardens between nine rungs,
eight meadow boxes, calendar
to their white hive, their damp
honey breath humming toward our light.

At Lost Lake

It was before we all could talk,
could only see, and listen.
At Lost Lake the family
camped in October.

There was a boat we gathered in,
went out over the water,
pointing to the light,
excited by it.

Then they took away
a board on the floor
and there was glass
all the way down.

Between us we looked
below the world, all
darker than the air
and still.

Then they put the board on,
we came to shore.
No-one needs
to go there again.

But when we gather,
sit together and talk,
we grow still
in each other's eyes—

we take the board away.

A Key to the Nature Library, 1909

What bird sings like a meadow grasshopper?
What bird is called *Whisky John* in the Adirondacks?
What is the great objection to a phoebe's nest
       in one's veranda?
What three purposes does the drumming tattoo of the
       downy woodpecker serve?
What is the crow's status in the opinion
       of intelligent farmers?
What claim has the cuckoo upon the farmer's good will?
What birds are conspicuously black?
What bird lines its nest with apple blossoms?
What bird has a love song that sounds like a dirge?
What outrageous habits have cow birds?
What bird has a sense of humor?
What birds were trained to fish in the days
       of John Milton?
What is the bob white's unique manner of sleeping?

What butterflies feed upon violets?
What butterflies hibernate?
What butterfly is a fighter?
Do fossil butterflies differ greatly from living forms?
Are caterpillars easily frozen to death?
What is the walnut case-bearer's little game?
How does the leopard moth pass its youth?
What is the intelligence of ants?
Who are the great students of ants?
What crimes has modern science laid at the door
       of flies and mosquitoes?
What insects have their ears in their elbows?

Under the North Eave

I attack the wasps with a vacuum cleaner—
I too have a sting, and I duck, bob and weave
as they come spiraling down to find me
when suddenly their wind is changed
to a vacancy departing, a tube from summer
to hell, and they fall headlong.

But now I have fifty-seven wasps inside
when I turn it off, abuzz
in the lint-ball mayhem of the bag
and surely starting their long climb
out the hose to skitter down the chrome
shaft and find me. My dreams
will never be the same: house of paper,
wings of cellophane, midnight honey of revenge.

Having Words With Belle

When honeysuckle sealed her screen door shut
she waved away my pruning shears.
"My pleasures are few," she said.
Bees hummed in the vine-cool shade.

I looked back where ropes of blossoms
knotted the whole facade, how
her house smouldered yellow
at the end of her slender road.

Pocatello Light

Came home late from working the plain
human world, from standing on the Benton
overpass above that small crooked house
with a garden and a dog. I saw
two tiny shoes on the doorstep.
I saw rows of sunflowers
bowing east for dawn, the whole
tribe's underwear and shirts hung
white in starlight between two steel poles.
And on the wall I saw a window lit
from within by a battered
table, by two hands closed
on one another.

You would be in the third-floor
dim hall of the Fargo,
would know how the charge builds
as I shuffle down the long carpet
to share the small spark that flashes
blue between our lips.

He Meant to Live

on the island without a road
in the house without a phone
or door. He meant to tell us
how to carry out our lives
back here on mainland ground.
He tucked those letters in
against his chest and roared
away too fast, for all the noise
of the crash too silent still
under the bridge, under rain
that owns his island, rain
that keeps track of distances,
marks out his vine-clamped
house, its rooms, one here
in my heart, one in yours.

Near Minerva

Vera sings her old song, its tune
a child voice in any throat
words thrill. We cross the pasture
filled with queen anne's lace
and yarrow, herb of gentle birth,
most graceful seed. From the west
a hill's shadow nets us with one sweep.

> *round and round the valley*
> *as we have done before*

Home is where you know your way
by dark. We follow the corridor
of cherry trees gone wild for years,
low boughs sweeping the grass,
trunks woven with honeysuckle.
Here the cat and owl died
in each other's claws.
No more night songs:

> *in and out the windows*
> *as we have done before*

The house shrouded by blackberry:
arch of thorn, shorn blossom, white-back
leaves. Nettles numb our ankles. Bats
whisper against the sky for bugs, where stars
tingle behind their wings. The knob
comes off in Leo's hand. "Can you find
the ice-pick key, my dear?"

> *stand and face your lover*
> *as we have done before*

Fire kindled, alder burns eagerly.
Flame through chinks in the stove
lights a patch of his hand, brightens

her hair. We must be long together.

follow me to London
as we have done before

"They say Minerva was a farmer's wife.
They say the Meadows brothers built
that covered bridge, condemned in
thirty-nine, still trusted. I've heard
the horse that runs from our approach
hasn't been ridden for years. How
will we be loving here, where
isolation turns everything wild?"
A spark jumps and orphaned kittens
stare into the fire.

kiss her before you leave her
as we have done before

A Kaiser slumps in the drive.
From here the road goes by faith
in the creek it follows: there will be
a way, a slender way between
dark hills. We follow by the sound
of our steps. Stars hard as gravel
under our shoes keep turning:

round and round the valley
as we have done before

Beautiful Old Wreck

It's easy to forgive a rig for trouble
if you give her a name. The Duchess—now
there was a car! My brother gave her up
when he moved to the island. Buried in snow
all winter, eighteen below, she started
and she hummed with the key's first turn
and drove tough miles, here to the moon.
Anyone gets tired, anyone gets frayed
and windows won't open, doors won't close,
and mushrooms knob the rug where that leak
kept on. But dear, old girl, when we
traded the keys for a few lousy bucks
to that cruel mechanic in the trailer park,
I prayed for your soul.

All

Possession is a weight, physical
simply—all love just this:
a second body we feel we need:
woman, husband, daughter, son.

My child, my child, my child
I help you simply, a lump
drawn from my weight—
my lovely bloom
who from the stem would go
drifting abrupt from reach
until my hands and body
nearly tore from themselves
to take you back, back, and
back.
      But then I withered
as you grew or died or
disappeared into a stranger
older than the one I shed
(retreating inward, weightless
as a seed).
          Oh Summer, Autumn,
Susan, Gabriel, May—which
name was it that I chose?
Which name did you become,
and live through, and leave
before I saw it carved on stone?

My little oat, awkward as wind
in my arms when I lay you down
for sleep, let this be my saying
for you, once you are born, once
you are mine, then free,
forgetting who made the song
that made itself.

Tears of the Slot-Eyed Child

In the Palace of Nature I was prey
gazing back at the two-headed gopher snake
caged in glass, its lazy skeleton
rippling scale by scale over lettuce
the wilted hand of its keeper held out:
one hunger, two mouths.

By night writhing in my arms our
daughter's first head of pain from its
soft spine swivels up slowly
while something not digested
knots her belly, and her cry
forks out to stun my heart.

By day her second head laughs
and learns a word or charm
accidentally perfect: a wonder
she can live as one this long
when darkness tucks away her bright
intelligible face, and the terrible
first suffering head rises
over the cribside speaking
one syllable.

Walking to the Mailbox

We found a turtle stunned by sunlight
dozing easy with half-shut eyes,
and as I bent down, my little Rosemary,
strapped to my back, stirred and
murmured. When I held its knobbed green
body up, her quick breath moistened
my ear, while the turtle, dazed
by eternity, made perfect unto itself
by so many million years, looked
back at my little one, all wisdom
and danger, trouble and delight
unfurled in the slots of its yellow eyes.

Hunched on the ground again it broke
from its trance, sinewy legs
reaching out, the green skull
of itself tottering slowly away,
made strong by wearing its
own death outward as I did
rising up with Rosemary.

Joanne's Gift

At dawn Joanne heard mule colt
bray and went to feed it. Down
Smith River road a single foxglove
bloom whizzed past, grazing her shoulder
to skid and quiver in the rut. By her
shoe the bruised bloom throbbed, flower
with a black slim stem that buzzed. She
plucked off ragged purple to find
a ruby-throat feather thumb
hummingbird kindle the light
and be gone.

Years later, as she rubbed the grown
mule's ear at dusk, she told us
how these seasons care for her,
how good neighbors leave her wood
and bread, how sweet the taste,
her cup of water.

Back Home in the Shopping Center

I found the corner where children ride
the worn plastic horse leaping on its post,
tail adrift, saddle horn dark from desperate sweat,
leather reins jingling with chrome—but now
so still, so still it made me lonely
for a quarter, for a body small enough
to clamber into the gum-studded saddle
tooled with roses, to kick the red spur
so the pony rolls and champs its bit,
runs away, muzak whinnying,
other mothers turning to see
who squalls from that wobbling steed
blasting for the sage. Oh centuries,
you are so little for human joy.